THE
END
OF
IGNORANCE

INTRODUCTION

This is no ordinary book.

The first thing you will notice is it is written by hand.

This is intentional. In this impersonal, technologically constructed world full of Times New Roman and like buttons, we have contact with more information, but less substance. There is power in handwriting. It is real, it is human, it is vulnerable.

My handwriting is far from perfect, and even my punctuation and grammar have room for improvement, and I am OK with that. Because these words come from my heart.

This is a handwritten note to you. I want you to feel like you know me, through the shapes of my letters and my human errors. I hope this nontraditional gesture brings you a little closer to feeling connected — to me, but even more so, to you.

This book is about the power of your mind. Consider it mental training, following a simple A to Z outline, designed to improve the quality of your life. Maybe you'll think this is crazy or silly. But however you feel about it, hear that very thought in your head, as an observer, and realize that impression does not define you, no more than it defines this book. Your mind is streaming a nonstop playlist of information and what you put into it are the songs it will play back.

It's like the old Cherokee legend about "the two wolves." As the story goes; a wise Cherokee man is teaching his grandson about life. "A fight is always going on inside me," he explains. "A fight between two wolves. One is evil. He is anger, resentment, sadness, envy, greed, guilt, doubt. The other is good: joy, peace, confidence, trust, truth, compassion, generosity. The same fight is going on inside you, too." The boy asks his grandfather, "So which wolf will win?" The old man answers, "Whichever wolf you feed." This stands true for all of us. But I believe this ancient legend is incomplete. It doesn't explain what kind of food to feed the wolf. It doesn't tell you where to find the food, how much food, how often to feed it or what is the best kind of food for the wolf.

This book finishes the important story of the two wolves. It clearly outlines exactly the best way to nourish the good wolf living inside you. Everybody understands if you put gas into your car, it will drive you to wherever you want to go. If you put Coke in your tank, it won't get you anywhere. Your mind is an even more powerful vehicle and it drives on what you feed it.

This book is packed with simple, nutritious fuel for your life. You see, everything is created twice: First in your mind, then in the world around you. The four-minute mile used to be considered impossible; your heart would explode if you even got close. Then someone did it. The impossible became possible because someone first thought, "I think I can do that." If you can step away from and rise above your existing, limiting thoughts and judgments, you will experience this incredible fact: This book will change your life, if you want it to. This book is for anyone who wants to live a better life.

For years, I have created thousands of workouts to help people get into physical shape. Now, I have created a workout for the mind that does the equivalent of what my fitness exercises do for the body. I understand that life can be tough. Like you, I have had to make the choice to be bigger than challenges and focus on a greater good. I have felt pain, too. I was molested throughout my youth by the foster kids I lived with. I lost my brother to drugs at age 12, and my mom died when I was only 20. This is just the beginning of the hardships I have been struck with. Yet I still find a way to wake up every day with a smile and gratitude for life.

Although it hasn't been an easy journey, it is by following this A to Z recipe that I have been able to live every day to the fullest. I have it memorized and live it out daily. I've been there. I've suffered. I've helped others have fitness success by using these same principles. You can and will have success with this program, too. Anyone can do this.

Follow the steps A to Z, every day. See how many letters you can get. Or if you feel overwhelmed with attempting all 26 letters every day, just highlight one letter each day for 26 days. Each letter represents a word, and each word connects with a positive thought. For each thought, I offer you a quick and easy action to take. And if you want further inspiration, I also provide an inspirational song, quote and book to read for each letter.

Peace
Love
Happiness
Infintite Abundance

— I am

ATTITUDE

ONE THING YOU HAVE COMPLETE CONTROL OVER ☺

CHOOSE A <u>GREAT</u>

ATTITUDE ☺

☮ ♡ ☺

Action: Smile + count to 20 million ☺
1 million, 2 million ... 20 million

Song: Happy ☺
♡Pharrell♡

Book: Man's Search for Meaning ☺
♡Viktor Frankl♡

Quote: People may hear your words, but they feel your attitude ☺
♡John Maxwell♡

B

BREATH

THE MOST IMPORTANT THING IN YOUR LIFE ☺
WITHOUT IT EVERYTHING ELSE WILL DISAPPEAR ☺

BREATHE CONSCIOUSLY ☺

☮ ♡ ☺

Action: Inhale + Exhale 10x :)

Inhale: All that is good :)
Exhale: Everything else

Song: Breathe :) ♡Faith Hill♡

Book: The Untethered Soul :) ♡Michael Singer♡

Quote: Life is not measured by the number of breaths we take, but the moments that take our breath away :) ♡Maya Angelou♡

☮ ♡ :)

CONFIDENCE

BELIEVING IS THE FIRST STEP IN ACHIEVING ANY GOAL ☺

BE CONFIDENT ☺

ACTION: Say outloud "I THINK, I CAN!" 10x :)

SONG: Roar :)
♡ Katy Perry ♡

BOOK: You are a Badass :)
♡ Jen Sincero ♡

QUOTE: When you want to succeed as bad as you want to breathe, then you'll be successful :)
♡ Eric Thomas ♡

☮ ♡ :)

D

DETERMINATION

THE ONLY WAY TO FAIL IS TO STOP TRYING :)

BE <u>DETERMINED</u> :)

Action: Say outloud "Can't stop, won't stop" 10x ☺

Song: Eye of the Tiger ☺ ♡Survivor♡

Book: The Compound Effect ☺ ♡Darren Hardy♡

Quote: Success is going from failure to failure whitout losing enthusiasm ☺ ♡Winston Churchill♡

EXERCISE

Your body loves it, so do more of it ☺

Exercise Daily ☺

☮♡☺

ACTION: 15 or more min/day Follow TrainerJoe for daily workouts ☺

SONG: Good Vibrations ☺ ♡Marky Mark♡

BOOK: Take The Stairs ☺ ♡Rory Vaden♡

QUOTE: An object in motion will stay in motion ☺ ♡Isaac Newton♡

F

FAITH

You are the contractor of your life, and your faith is the foundation you will build upon ☺

Have a **Strong** Faith ☺

☮ ♡ ☺

Action: Close your eyes + say your faith out loud ☺

Song: The Strangest Secret ☺ ♡Earl Nightingale♡

Book: You've Got to Stand for Something ☺ ♡Aaron Tippin♡

Quote: Build your house on the rock, because it will rain, flood, and blow in life, and a house built on the rock will still stand ♡Jesus♡

☮ ♡ ☺

G

GRATITUDE

BE THANKFUL FOR WHAT YOU HAVE TODAY, IN PREPARATION FOR WHAT TOMORROW WILL BRING ☺

BE <u>GRATEFUL</u> ☺

☮ ♡ ☺

ACTION: LIST 10 THINGS YOU'RE THANKFUL FOR ☺

1.   4.   7.
2.   5.   8.   THIS
3.   6.   9.   10. MOMENT
                  ☮ ♡ ☺

SONG: WHAT A WONDEFUL WORLD ☺
♡ LOUIS ARMSTRONG ♡

BOOK: THE GIVING TREE ☺
♡ SHEL SILVERSTEIN ♡

QUOTE: TRADE YOUR EXPECTATION TO APPRECIATION AND THE WORLD CHANGES INSTANTLY ☺
♡ TONY ROBBINS ♡

☮ ♡ ☺

HELP OTHERS

Serving others brings more joy + fulfillment than any other activity :)

Be Helpful :)

ACTION: Offer 1 or more person help/day ☺
'May I help you' ☺

SONG: Lean on Me ☺
♡ Bill Withers ♡

BOOK: The Energy Bus ☺
♡ Jon Gordon ♡

QUOTE: Love your neighbor as yourself, no command is greater than these ☺
♡ Jesus ♡

IMAGINATION

Everything in life is created twice; first, in your mind, second, in the physical world ☺

Dream Big ☺

☮ ♡ ☺

ACTION: List 3 ideas to improve life/day ☺

1.   2.   3.

SONG: Somewhere Over the Rainbow ☺
♡Brother IZ♡

BOOK: Think & Grow Rich ☺
♡Napoleon Hill♡

QUOTE: All our dreams can come true if we have the courage to pursue them ☺
♡Walt Disney♡

J

JOKE

We all make mistakes, laugh at yourself, learn the lesson + move on :)

Be Light Hearted :)

ACTION: LOL :)
SERIOUSLY! DO IT :)

SONG: Shake It Off :)
♡ Taylor Swift ♡

BOOK: Choose Yourself :)
♡ James Altucher ♡

QUOTE: If your compassion does not include <u>yourself</u>, it is incomplete :)
♡ Buddha ♡

☮ ♡ :)

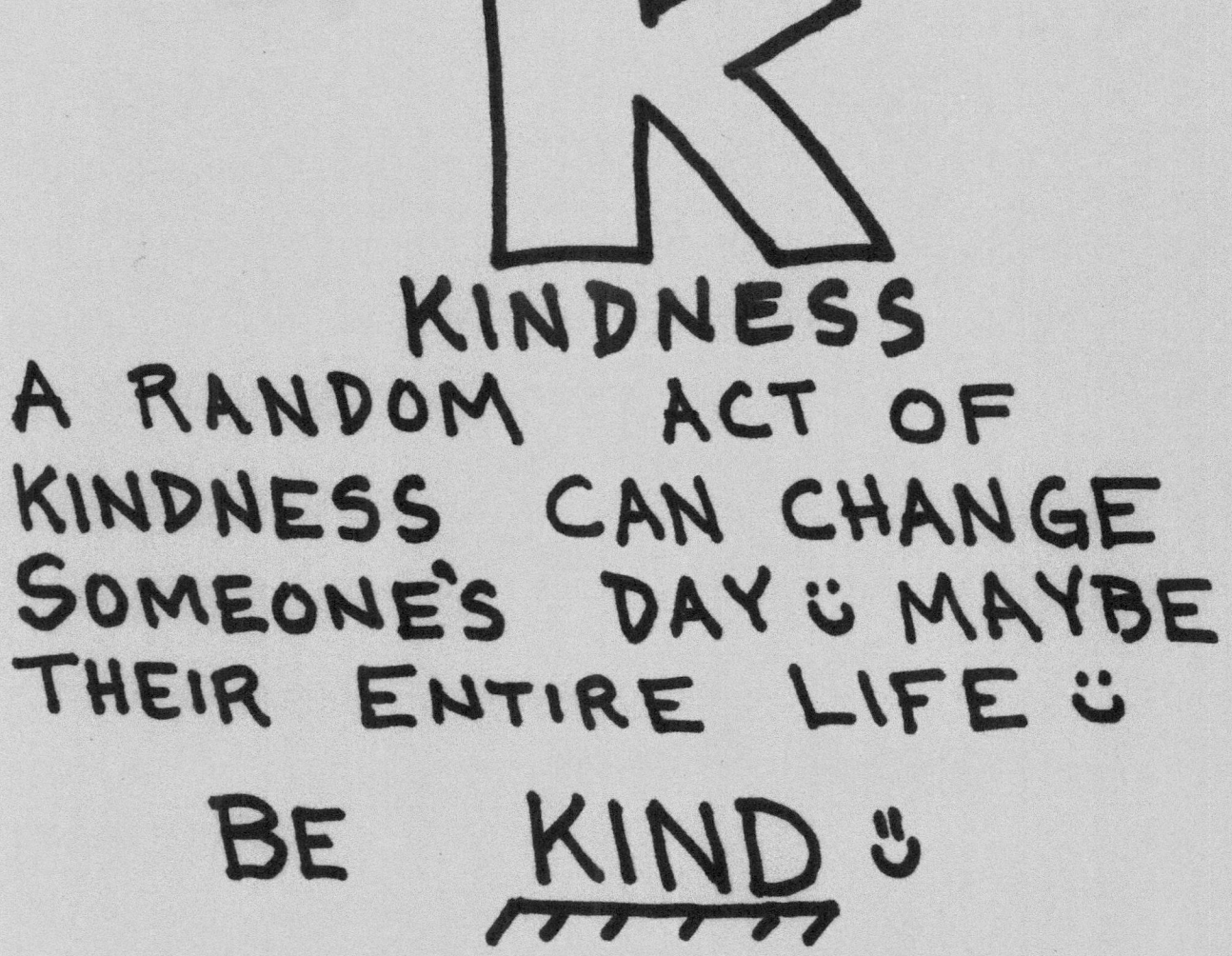

ACTION: Give 1 or more sincere complements/day
"You are so beautiful" ☺
☮♡☺

SONG: Don't let the sun go down on me ☺
♡ Elton John ♡

BOOK: How to win Friends & Influence People ☺
♡ Dale Carnegie ♡

QUOTE: It's amazing what doors can open if you reach out to people with a smile, friendly attitude & desire to make a positive impact ☺
♡ Sir Richard Branson ♡

☮ ♡ ☺

Love

A GIFT THAT IS FREE TO GIVE, + PRICELESS WHEN RECEIVED ☺

BE <u>Love</u> ♡

Action: Say outloud "I Love Myself!" 20x ☺

Song: Love is my Religion ☺ ♡ Ziggy Marley ♡

Book: The 5 Love Languages ☺ ♡ Gary Chapman ♡

Quote: Love is patient, Love is kind, it doesn't envy, it doesn't boast, it is not proud, it doesn't dishonor others, it is not self seeking, it is not easily angered, it keeps no record of wrong. Love doesn't delight in evil but rejoices with the truth. Love always protects, trusts, hopes, persevers ☺ ♡ Paul ♡

☮ ♡ ☺

M

MANIFEST

You get what you think about most of the time ☺

Think Positively ☺
=================

☮ ♡ ☺

Action: Write out your desires daily ☺

☮ ♥ ☺

Song: Don't Stop Believin'
♥ Journey ♥

Book: The Secret ☺
♥ Rhonda Byrne ♥

Quote: What you think about you bring about ☺
♥ Lisa Nichols ♥

☮ ♥ ☺

N
NUTRITION

You are what you eat :)

FUEL UP PROPERLY :)

☮ ♡ ☺

Action: Gluten Free ☺
Sugar Free

Song: Apples + Bananas ☺
♡Raffi♡

Book: Body For Life ☺
♡Bill Phillips♡

Quote: Our food should be our medicine and our medicine should be our food ☺
♡Hippocrates♡

①

OPEN MINDED

WE ALL HAVE OUR OWN IDEAS ☺ HAVE THE ABILITY TO RECOGNIZE THEY ARE NOT THE ONLY ONES ☺

BE <u>OPEN MINDED</u> ☺

☮ ♡ ☺

Action: Feel the top of your head ☺

Song: We Are The World ☺ ♥U.S.A. for Africa♥

Book: The Power of Now ☺ ♥Eckhart Tolle♥

Quote: There is nothing either good or bad, but thinking makes it so ☺ ♥Shakespeare♥

☮♥☺

P

PURPOSE

YOU ARE THE CAPTAIN OF YOUR LIFE :) + YOUR PURPOSE IS THE MAP TO THE GREATEST TREASURE IN THE UNIVERSE :)

LIVE WITH PURPOSE :)

☮ ♡ ☺

ACTION: Say outloud your purpose ☺
My purpose in life is to...

SONG: It's my life ☺
♡ Bon Jovi ♡

BOOK: Good to Great ☺
♡ Jim Collins ♡

QUOTE: The meaning of life is to find your gift, the purpose of life is to give it away ☺
♡ Picasso ♡

Q

QUIET TIME

REMOVE LIFE'S MENTAL + PHYSICAL DISTRACTIONS AND FIND PEACE + STILLNESS WITHIN ☺

MEDITATE DAILY ☺

☮ ♡ ☺

ACTION: 15 or more min/day sit in stillness with eyes closed ☺ a.k.a. MEDITATE ☺

SONG: Rhapsody in Blue ☺ ♡George Gershwin♡

BOOK: The 7 Laws of Spiritual Success ☺ ♡Deepak♡

QUOTE: Your vision will become clear when you can look into your own heart. Who looks outside dreams, who looks inside awakes ☺ ♡Carl Jung♡

☮ ♡ ☺

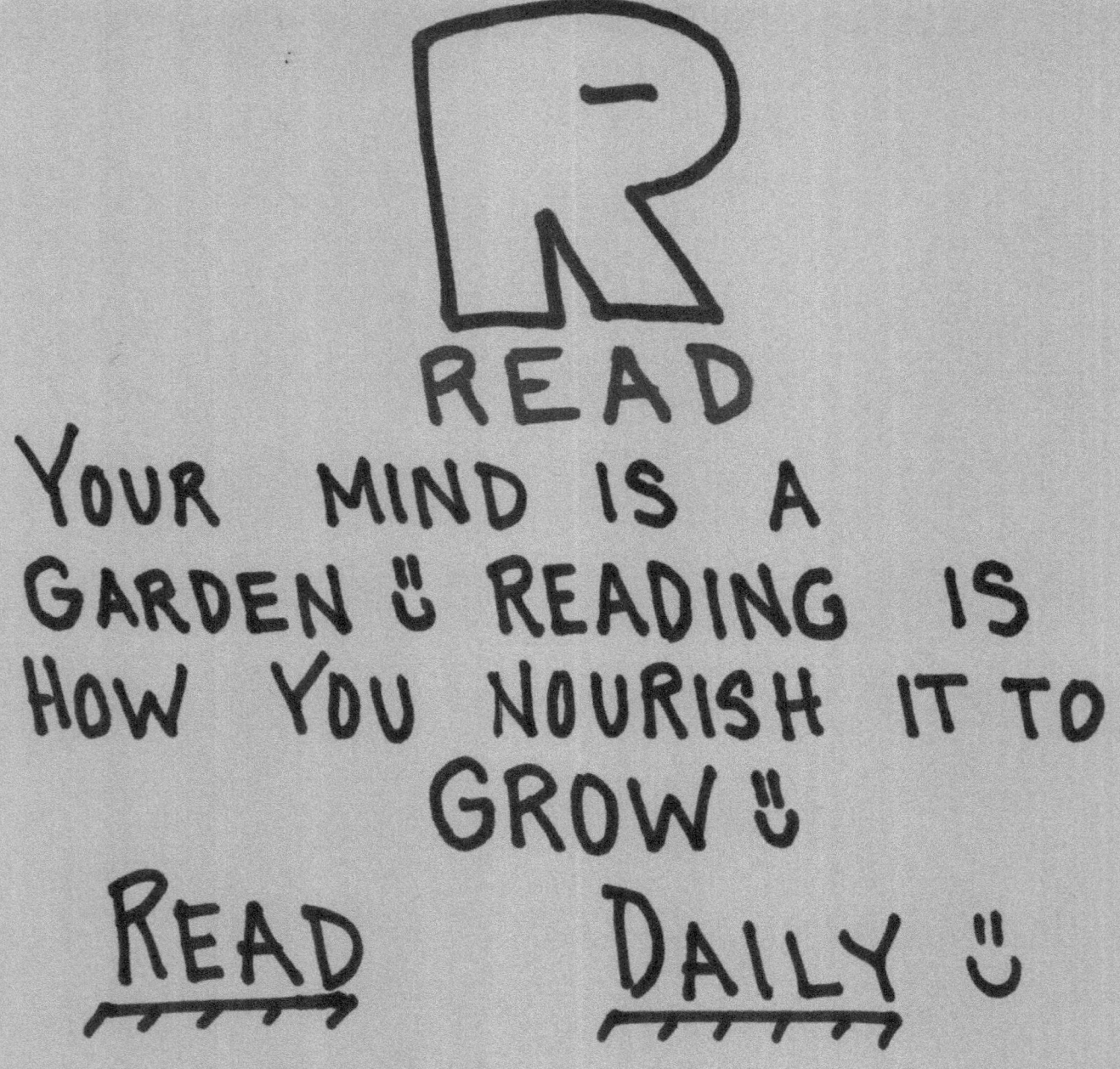

ACTION: 15 or more min/day read a book on improvement :)

SONG: Reading Rainbow Theme Song :) ♥Reading Rainbow♥

BOOK: Total Money Makeover :) ♥Dave Ramsey♥

QUOTE: What we think, we create
What we feel, we attract
What we imagine, we become.

♥Buddha♥

💤 SLEEP

Your body needs time to recharge ☺ Get quality, consistent sleep. SLEEP PEACEFULLY ☮

ACTION: 7 hours of sleep or more/day

SONG: Imagine :)
♡ John Lennon ♡

BOOK: Goodnight Moon :)
♡ Margaret Wise Brown ♡

QUOTE: Early to bed, early to rise, makes a man (woman) healthy, wealthy, and wise :)
♡ Benjamin Franklin ♡

☮ ♡ ✌

T
TOUCH

The Universal Healing Power ☺

Touch Those Around You!!

☮ ♥ ☺

ACTION: Give 1 or more HUGS per day :)

SONG: Butterfly Kisses :) ♡Bob Carlisle♡

BOOK: Love Yourself Like Your Life Depends On It :) ♡Kamal Ravikant♡

QUOTE: We touch other people's lives simply by existing :) ♡J. K. Rowling♡

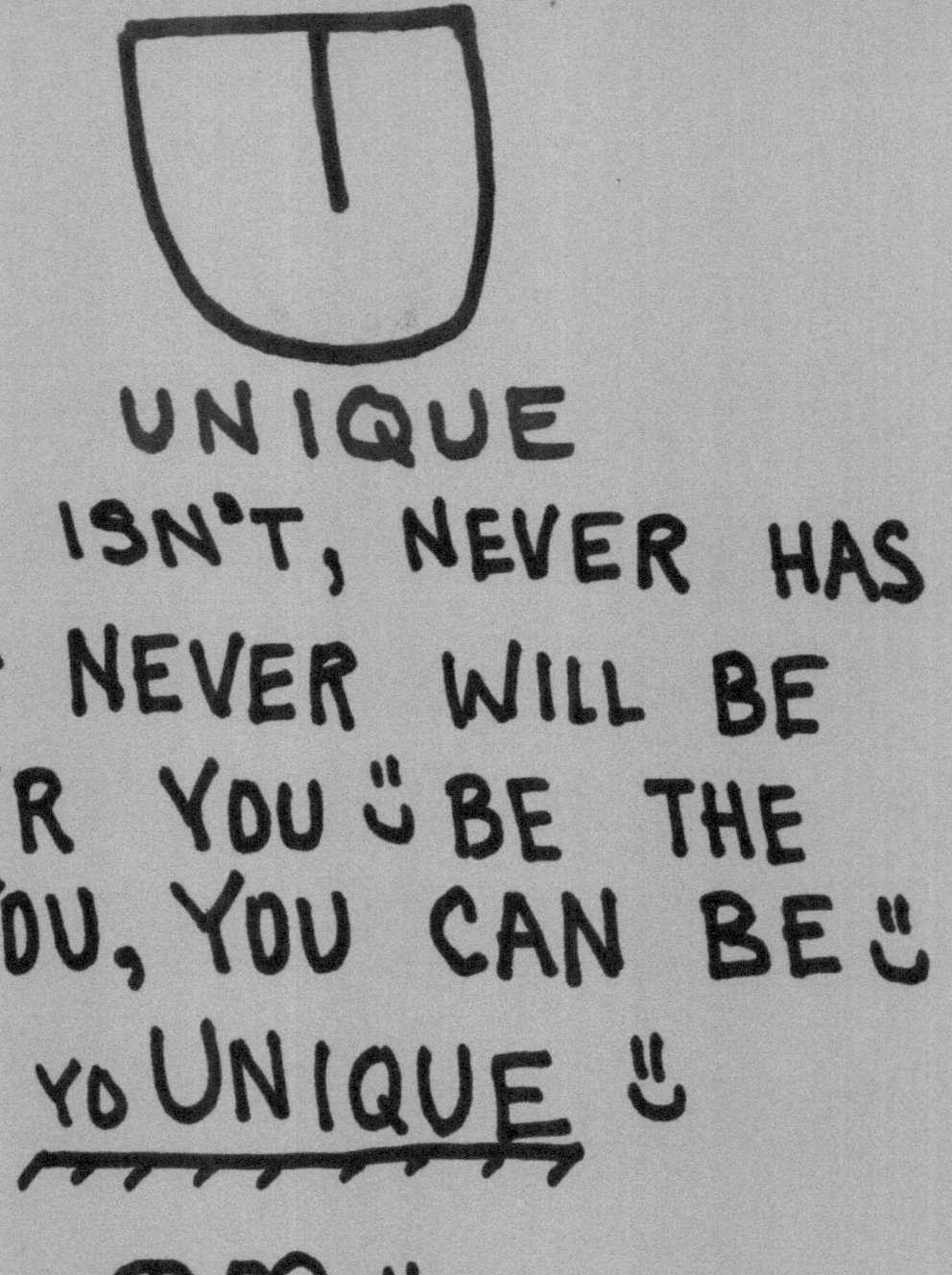

UNIQUE

THERE ISN'T, NEVER HAS BEEN, + NEVER WILL BE ANOTHER YOU :) BE THE BEST YOU, YOU CAN BE :)

BE <u>YoUNIQUE</u> :)

ACTION: Say outloud who YOU want to be from A to Z ☺

A - Amazing, B - Brave................Z - Zen

SONG: Man in the mirror ☺
♡ Michael Jackson ♡

BOOK: Presence ☺
♡ Amy Cuddy ♡

QUOTE: Today you are you, that is truer than true ☺ There is no one alive who is youer than YOU ☺
♡ Dr. Seuss ♡

V

VISUALIZE

WHAT YOU SEE IS WHAT YOU GET ☺

<u>VISUALIZE</u> <u>SUCCESS</u> ☺

ACTION: Close your eyes + visualize your manifestations ☺

SONG: Where the Streets Have No Name ☺ ♥U2♥

BOOK: Awaken the Giant Within ☺ ♥Tony Robbins♥

QUOTE: Everything is energy + that's all there is to it ☺ Match the frequency of the reality you want + you can not help but get that reality. It can be no other way ☺ This is not philosophy ☺ This is physics ☺   ♥Einstein♥

W
WATER

You're made of it, so drink more of it :)

Hydrate <u>Feel</u> <u>Great</u> :)

☮ ♡ ☺

ACTION: DRINK 0.75 oz × IDEAL BODY WEIGHT

i.e. 0.75 [IBW] = ___ oz

SONG: SAILING ☺
♡ CHRISTOPHER CROSS ♡

BOOK: BE LIKE WATER ☺
♡ JOSEPH CARDILLO ♡

QUOTE: YOU MUST BE SHAPELESS, FORMLESS LIKE WATER ☺ WHEN YOU POUR WATER IN A CUP IT BECOMES A CUP, WHEN YOU POUR WATER IN A BOTTLE IT BECOMES A BOTTLE, WHEN YOU POUR WATER IN A TEAPOT IT BECOMES A TEAPOT, WATER CAN DRIP + IT CRASHES. BECOME LIKE WATER MY FRIEND ☺
♡ BRUCE LEE ♡

X

X-RAY VISION

Look past life's facades and see the beauty within ☺

Have X-RAY VISION ☺

ACTION: Forgive 1 or more person/day :)

SONG: The Heart of the Matter ~ Don Henley ~

BOOK: The 4 Agreements ~ Don Miguel Ruiz ~

QUOTE: If people knew better, they would do better :) ♡ OPRAH ♡

☮ ♡ :)

ACTION: Touch Your Toes ☺
It's the only place you can be ☺

SONG: The River
♡ Garth Brooks ♡

BOOK: The Alchemist ☺
♡ Paulo Coelho ♡

QUOTE: The Journey is the Reward ☺
♡ Steve Jobs ♡

☮ ♡ ☺

Z
ZEAL

Because a good life is the only life worth living!!

Welcome to your <u>Life</u> :)

☮ ♡ ☺

ACTION: Put your hands in the air + smile ☺ This is your life story ☺

SONG: Feeling Good ☺ ♡ Michael Buble ♡

BOOK: See You at the Top ☺ ♡ Zig Ziglar ♡

QUOTE: When I was 5, my mom always told me that happiness was the key to life ☺ When I went to school they asked me what I wanted to be when I grew up ☺ I wrote down 'Happy' ☺ They told me I didn't understand the assignment, I told them they didn't understand LIFE ☺ ♡ John Lennon ♡

The Key To A More Enjoyable Quality of Life From A to Z

A-Z	Word	Action	Check
A	Attitude	Smile & Count to 20 Million :)	
B	Breath	Inhale &Exhale 10x :)	
C	Confidence	Say 'I Think, I Can!' 10x :)	
D	Determination	Say 'Can't Stop, Won't Stop!' 10x :)	
E	Exercise	15 Minutes or More :)	
F	Faith	Close Your Eyes and State Your Faith :)	
G	Gratitude	List 10 Things You're Thankful For :)	
H	Help Others	Offer 1 or More Person Help :)	
I	Imagination	List 3 Ideas to Improve Life :)	
J	Joke	Laugh Out Loud :)	
K	Kindness	Give 1 or More Sincere Complements :)	
L	Love	Say 'I Love Myself!' 20x :)	
M	Manifest	Write Out Your Desires :)	
N	Nutrition	Gluten Free, Sugar Free :)	
O	Open-minded	Feel The Top of Your Head :)	
P	Purpose	Say Your Purpose :)	
Q	Quiet Time	15 Minutes or More Sit in Stillness With Eyes Closed :)	
R	Read	15 Minutes or More :)	
S	Sleep	7 Hours or More :)	
T	Touch	Give 1 or More Hugs :)	
U	Unique	Say Who You Want to Be From A to Z :)	
V	Visualize	Close Your Eyes & Visualize Your Manifestations :)	
W	Water	Drink 0.75oz x Ideal Body Weight :)	
X	X-Ray Vision	Forgive 1 or More Person :)	
Y	YOGA	Touch Your Toes :)	
Z	Zeal	Put Your Hands in The Air & Smile :)	

THE BEGINNING
OF
☮ ♥ ☺!!

www.ingramcontent.com/pod-product-compliance
Lightning Source LLC
Chambersburg PA
CBHW040003080526
44586CB00027B/2866